ISBN 978-0-243-30032-7
PIBN 10792700

1 MONTH OF
FREE
READING

at

www.ForgottenBooks.com

By purchasing this book you are eligible for one month membership to ForgottenBooks.com, giving you unlimited access to our entire collection of over 1,000,000 titles via our web site and mobile apps.

To claim your free month visit:

www.forgottenbooks.com/free792700

THE PRIMITIVE BAPTIST.

B. TEMPLE, *EDITOR.* } "COME OUT OF HER, MY PEOPLE." { **N. W. POOLE,** *PRINTER.*

Vol. 22. *Milburnie, N. C., July* 10, 1858. No. 13.

NOTICE!

☞ *A New Post Office—A Change!!*

Having obtained a new Post Office nearer to us than heretofore, (Jordan S. Williams, P. M.,) our subscribers, friends and exchanges will please address us in the future at "*Milburnie, Wake County, North Carolina,*" and not at "Eagle Rock, N. C." "*Milburnie*" is nearer to us and we can have more frequent access to the Office than heretofore.

The Law of Newspapers.

1st, Subscribers who do not give express notice to the contrary, are considered wishing to continue their subscription.

2nd. If subscribers order a discontinuance of their papers, the publisher may continue to send them until all cash charges are paid.

3rd. If subscribers neglect or refuse to take their papers from the office to which they are directed, they are held responsible until they have settled their bill, and ordered their papers discontinued.

4th. If subscribers move to other places, without informing the publisher, and their paper is sent to the former direction, they are held responsible.

5th. The Courts have decided, that refusing to take a paper or periodical from the office, or removing and leaving it uncalled for, is *prima facie* evidence of intentional fraud.

COMMUNICATIONS.

For the Primitive Baptist.

BROTHER TEMPLE:—

I was born in the date of 1835, the 10 of June.—My mother died when I was eight years old, and my father when I was sixteen.—And when I look back and take a retrospective view of my life from seven years old up to the present, I am constrained to cry out,

"It is grace that has brought me thus far,
And grace will lead me home."

In my seventeenth year, I dreamed of seeing an old house and seven or eight persons outside drinking, in the dark, out of a small bottle, and the Devil came out at the door and marched them around me without one word being spoken to my hearing; and seeing they were under his control and so easily governed, I was made to fear and tremble, for I saw no way to escape. But in a way I did not expect, there appeared a member of the Baptist Church (his name was EMANUELL,) with me, and I sat between his feet until the crowd marched in the old house and turning to the left hand, down they went through the floor into a pit without bottom, one after the other; and I heard their shrieks and groans going down, down into that death, (which I think is the penalty of the law that the whole human family are born under and will die under, except they stand on that dear Friend who said "the gates of hell shall not prevail,") and I saw the smoke boil out as they sank down, and when they had sunk out of my hearing, Emanuell said unto me, "Now you see where you would have been if it had not been for me." Yes, it was grace bestowed on a wretch—the reason why he loved me, I cannot tell. I have cried, He has suffered and died to redeem my poor soul from hell, and brought me with him to dwell.

When I awoke, though it was a dream, it had a powerful effect on my mind; so from that time I, with my heart, soul and mind, tried to do good; but kept getting worse, even taking God's name in vain before I received faith in Jesus, or understood the plan. It was not but a few days after my dream, it came in my mind that I saw heaven and God sitting on his throne, and those in his presence all happily singing and praising: and all at a sudden a silence took place for about fifteen or twenty minutes—God justly calling for payment, and all were not able to satisfy nor find an equivalent to make reconciliation. I looked up at God, as I thought, and he smiled to see that they saw their weakness and ignorance, and at last their dependence on him. While in this giving-up situation, I saw an humble-looking man appear from a secret room on the right hand, and came round in front of the throne and walked up and reached out his hand and received a little book out of God's hand and walked down straight in the front away off out of sight;— that moment all things were praising and rejoicing as happily as they were before; but I could only think that was to let the world stand and give all a chance in this world, for I verily

thought if it had not been for that man coming up and taking that book, time would have ceased, and all would have perished, and that justly, too. Then my mother died, and I thought she was good and was gone home to heaven, and I was left so that if I would do good while in this world, when I died I could go to heaven also, and if I neglected to be good I should miss. So I tried to be good, but when I would get mad I would say things I was sorry for, but could not help it at the time when mad. I thought if I kept getting worse until I become grown, I should get to cursing; and if so, and could not help it when mad, I promised myself I would say, "Devil-damn you!"

After this my father died and the family all squandered.—I was like the lonesome dove,—I had lost a kind father and a good mother, and was now turned in the world to look out for self, and it seemed that every body was for self. Then I was taken and had the white-swelling for about two years, but it pleased God to raise me up again. As I strengthened in body, I saw that I was possessed of the same temper and instead of getting better, rather grew worse; and arrived to that point that I feared I should when I was a boy, and that was, cursing when provoked, and laid that and all that vexed me to the Devil, and thought because he could vex me when at my work, it was his trick in aggravating me; for I thought if I had nothing to do he could not vex me so, and I promised the Lord that, when I obtained a house and home, I would show him I would not work when I got mad, and would show that if I was working on my own farm, I would stop and sacrifice my work rather than to please the Devil so in cursing when things worked contrary. But I never thought it could be possible for me to have a family, for I had not sense enough to control and to be the head of one; it looked utterly impossible, but so it happened, I obtained a home and family, and went on for awhile. One very warm and dry day in July, I dropped my hoe and went in full haste to the spring to get water, and as I stepped to the edge of it I trod on a stick, one end of which lay in the water, and stirred it. I felt the ambition in me commence swelling like as though it were going to boil over; but I thought of the promise I had made before I obtained a home of my own, and I said to myself, I will see you out now, Devil—I will not curse—I will stand here all day first: so I put my hand on my mouth. About this time a frog slipped up the spout;—I clinched my lips with my fingers. In this time a couple of small puppies came up behind me, slipped and lay down in the spring, lapped the water and rolled their eyes up at me!—I was dared to move one foot, for I was swelled, apparently, as tought as a drum. At this time I commenced stifling for breath, for my nose seemed stopped up. I raised my hand off of my mouth just to breathe a little, and the breath that came through my lips came from my mouth with as pure a curse as though I had spoken it out in a laudible voice. I then, for the first time in my life, saw that I was a sinner; my very heart's nature was sinful; I was a mass of corruption; heart deceitful—desperately wicked. I had been trying to go to heaven, trusting this deceitful heart to work out a righteousness to justify itself in the sight of a just and holy God, and was not depending on Jesus no more than if there had been no Jesus. I was not looking for Jesus Christ's righteousness.

I at that time knew no more about the plan of salvation than a horse, but through necessity, feeling condemned, lost, miserable, blind, poor, naked and sinful, I had to go mourning my miserable condition. I had no body to blame but myself,—I was Bennet and Bennet—wrong Bennett—lost Bennet —a lost sinner—going wrong all the time, and was wrong for depending on that which was wrong.

Soon I lost my first child—seven months old to an hour; and when it died I grieved until I felt my heartstrings ache. I lay down on the bed and heard a voice, saying, This word shall come along again, and you shall know it. The voice was secret; it dried up my tears from grief; it seemed the hope of it brought it near, but I did not understand how it ever should come along. But the next time it spoke with that lovely voice; it was when I had almost lost sight of my troubles. About mid-night, the voice of the Son of God, as I hope, spoke to me and said, You shall understand right from wrong,—just as plain as the sun shines to-morrow. It had been cloudy three or four days before, but when the voice came, it awoke my soul and body. So I awoke my wife; told her what I had heard; I walked to the door and all was still; the very silence of creation seemed to be in obedience to God our Heavenly Father; the light seemed to light my soul with love; darkness banished. I walked back to the room, and the clock struck one, and it seemed to echo with as much solemnity as if the funeral and burial of some deceased notable character was being performed; I felt as though this world and its pleasures were nothing to compare with the company I had within me at that time. I feel it now while I am writing—that it is not gone out. I feel the love shed abroad in my heart without any thing to cause it that I ever done; it is a favor that God communes with the soul. Oh! that God, the Holy Ghost, would speak to me so again. I had rather hear his voice in mercy than to have all the world. People say there is no voice, but they say that because they have never heard it. If they ever hear the voice of the Son of God in his mercy, they will talk different. Then I had the *Primitive* reading, one day, and the plan of salvation opened to my mind—through Jesus and the necessity of his coming in the world and living and dying; though he was strong, yet became weak; performed that which our natures will not let us do, and went into death—conquered death, hell and the grave,—has arisen, and now promises when he speaks, and has the right to do so, for he has paid the debt of death, which we cannot satisfy.

I have just entered the best of my experience; but my sheet is full, so I will stop, by signing my name

B. P. PITT.

N. C., March 20, 1858.

For the Primitive Baptist.

BELOVED BRETHREN AND SISTERS:

I, even as unworthy as I am, through the tender mercies of HIM whose sceptre sways vast creation, have been protected and preserved thus far from diseases and death, and have been granted the privilege of seating myself to write a few lines for the perusal of the dear children of God scattered abroad over our land. And as I am blessed with a few leasure hours from the toil, labor and fatigue of my daily avocation, Oh! that my mind might be freed from the things pertaining to this poor world, or this mortal form which I carry about with me. For, dear brethren, the study for the good success and well-being of this old man

—flesh—keeps striving for the mastery; yea, and often has the advantage-ground so much so that I am made to cry, O, wretched man that I am, who shall deliver me from the body of this death! For to be carnally minded, we learn, is death; but to be spiritually minded is life. Then in the language of the poet I would say,—

Give me Thy Spirit, O my God!
  Then I can well all trials meet:
Deny myself and all my pride,
  And wash Thy weakest servant's
    feet."

Yes, dear brethren, how we should pray for the gift of His Spirit at all times, especially when we write for the columns of the *Primitive*, that we might not offend any of his little ones, but that we might comfort, console and edify the dear saints of God, whom Christ has purchased with his own blood.

Brethren, we learn that 'God is love,' and that 'he so loved the world that he gave his only begotten Son; that whosoever believed on him should not perish, but have everlasting life.' Again he says, "I have loved thee with an everlasting love, therefore with loving kindness have I drawn thee." Yes, brethren; and if we be drawn by the loving kindness of Almighty God, we will follow after him. If we have the love of God shed abroad in our hearts, our souls' desire is to walk in duty's paths. Then, brethren and sisters, in the books of the Old and New Testaments we have an infallible guide to our duty made so plain that the way-faring man, though a fool, cannot err therein.

Jesus said, "A new commandment I give unto you, That you love one another." Then if we have love one for another, "we know that we have passed from death unto life, because we love the brethren." "He that loveth not his brother, abideth in death: and by this we know that we love the children of God, When we love God and keep his commandments.". "If a man say, I love God, and hateth his brother, he is a liar: for he that loveth not his brother whom he hath seen, how can he love God whom he hath not seen?"

The above quoted scriptures, or passages of scripture, may not be quoted exactly correct, as my head is no concordance, nevertheless, they are to that amount, and present some of the evidence by which we may examine ourselves to see whether we be in the faith. Yea or nay, brethren, it is our duty to examine ourselves by the rule laid down in the scriptures. Hence, our Lord has said, "Search the scriptures, for in them ye think ye have eternal life, and they are they which testify of me." So we find that our Heavenly Father has not left us to guess at our duty, but it is written plainly in the Old and New Testaments; and 'whatsoever was written aforetime was written for our learning.' Then, brethren, our Bible is a Book of books, or far better than all other books, because it contains every thing necessary to our well-being, both in this world and the world to come.

Brethren and sisters, when I seated myself and commenced to try to write, I thought I would write some upon the christian duty—upon the christian duty towards God, towards the Church, and towards their fellow-creatures—sometimes called 'practical Godliness'; but it seems I have had to follow my mind, wandering as it is, and at last I am no nearer the subject than when I commenced. I wonder if any brother who pretends to write for the public eye feels his weakness so sensible as I do. So feeling my inability to do the subject justice, I will just say a few more words, in order to stir up your pure minds by way of remembrance, and leave this imperfect piece with brother Temple to dispose of as his better judgment may direct.

I would say to you, brethren and sisters, in the language of Paul, "As ye have therefore received Christ Jesus the Lord, so walk ye in him. Be ye all of one mind, having compassion one of another." Love as brethren; be pitiful; be courteous, remembering that whoso hath this world's goods and seeth his brother have need, and shutteth up his bowells of compassion from him, we are asked, How dwells the love of God in him? Then, brethren and sisters, if we have a name and a seat in the house of God, let us endeavor to let our light so shine that others seeing our good works may be constrained to glorify our Father which is heaven. Let us attend our conference meetings punctually, and not forsake the assembling of ourselves together. Let us visit the poor, widow and orphan, the sick and afflicted, and those in distressed circumstances and administer to their necessities as far as in our power. And while the world is expending fortunes to evangelize or convert the world, let the Church be engaged in her every duty as laid down in that book which she acknowledges as her only rule of faith and practice. So, dear brethren, farewell for the present, as my sheet is full, such as it is; but I assure you it is not less than its unworthy writer, who feels himself at times almost the very embodiment of imperfection.

Brother Temple, brethren and sisters, pray for unworthy me, that as I have enlisted in the cause of Christ that, like a good soldier, I may die at my post.

I remain, as ever your unworthy brother, in hope of a blest immortality,   WM. E. FREEMAN.

Ala., June 12, 1858.

For the Primitive Baptist

DEAR BROTHER TEMPLE:

Through the tender mercy of God bestowed on me, I am yet breathing the breath of life and enjoying good bodily health, and also in possession of that hope which maketh not ashamed, which hath for its object and centre-point Christ the Lord; and with this blessed hope in my soul I move along tolerably well, considering what a sin-disordered world this is and how depraved my nature. My Gospel enjoyments do not run very high, but still I am enabled to rest on, to confide in, to look to, and to make my boast of the Saviour of sinners, and it is from Him that I expect protection while here below.

I have been thinking of giving some of my thoughts about the 'elect lady' and her children, (2nd John i. 1.,) whom John said "he loved in the truth; and not I only, but also all they that have known the truth." Now I have to draw the bow at a venture, for I do not think I ever heard any body say any thing about the subject, public or private in my life. The word *lady* does not occur in Holy Writ but one time, but *truth* is in several places. We read that, 'the truth alone is to make men and women free.' Now, beloved, which is the best to contend for— the truth and be free, or for error and be a slave to all eternity? Think now and see where we stand; and if we are willing to confide in the truth alone from our hearts, and say like old Job, "I know that my Redeemer liveth."—Job. xix. 25. Now, do you not think that was the truth? We read that, 'none can say that Jesus is the Lord, but by the Holy Ghost.' I think that God, the Holy Ghost, finds or makes himself known to the heirs of promise. 1st John, iv. 4: "Ye are of God, little children;" not large children, no, but in their own eyes they look little indeed, I think,—and what is the reason? Because the Holy Ghost has taught them to feel little in deed and in truth. But read Luke 7th ch. 25th v: "But wisdom is justified of all her children."—Matt xi. 19. So we see that wisdom has children. Now, beloved, do you think these children are wisdom's and the elect lady whom John loved in the truth? One might say, I read in Judges v. 29, "her wise ladies." Yes, we have a plenty that have become wise above what is written, and we may not think it strange. Read Amos viii. 11: "Behold, the days come, saith the Lord God, that I will send a famine in the land, not a famine of bread, nor a thirst for water, but of hearing the words of the Lord." Says one, I hear the words of the Lord very frequently. What! in truth, the word? To hear, I think, is to obey; —Hear, O Israel, the Lord our God is one Lord. John said, "The hour is coming, and now is, when the dead shall hear the voice of the Son of God; and they that hear shall live." If the word *hear* was just the sound of something, you know that every body might hear that something, and Universalian doctrine would be right. But, sir, stop awhile and think, for we read, "Straight is the gate, and narrow is the way, that leadeth to life; and few there be which enter in thereat." You may find out this, reader, if you will try; read Rev. xxii. 14: "Blessed are they that do his commandments, that they may have right to the tree of life, and may enter in through the gates into the city." Now, beloved, you see that there is a people that has a right to go through the gates into the city—and why? Because they are his by gift,—and is this all? No; they are his by purchase, and therefore they delight to do his commandments. Do you think those that do not contend for the truth, have any right to the tree of life—when we read, The truth alone shall make poor sinners free? and as John seemed to have his eye upon a certain object, or in other words, upon the church, he tells us to "love one another;" 1st John iii. 23. "All thy children shall be taught of the Lord; and great shall be the peace of thy children;" Isa. liv. 13. Now, beloved, will God, or can he, who cannot lie, lay aside his justice and save people, when he said, My counsel shall stand, and I will do all my pleasure? Read the same chapter. Do you think God is like man—say one thing and do another? or tell a lie? If you do, what sort of a God do you have? one like man—say one thing and do another? or tell a lie? If you have, what sort of a God is he? Read Numbers xxiii. 19 : "God is not a man, that he should lie; neither the son of man, that he should repent: hath he said, and shall he not do it? or hath he spoken, and shall he not make it good?" So I believe, for one, that he is a God of purpose; a covenant-God, 'ordered in all things, and sure;' 2nd Sam'l. xxiii. 5. So I agree with David in a covenant-God, who will do all his pleasure. But we read that there was an 'unknown god,' (Acts xvii. 23,) yes, unknown to the heirs of promise; and we read (Psalms 144,) of 'strange children.' Well, we need not be startled at these, but let us 'stand fast in the liberty wherewith Christ hath made us free;' for Jerusalem, which is above, is free, is the mother of us all. We read Jesus said, "Sanctify them through thy truth: thy word is truth;" John xvii. 17; for the Lord said by Isa. lxvi. 9; ' Shall I bring to the birth, and not

cause to bring forth? saith the Lord: shall I cause to bring forth, and shut the womb? saith thy God." Now, beloved; if Zion has to travail before there can be children, do you not want to see that time come? I think I do. I often think and say within myself, When will the Lord's set time come to favor Zion? And although he seems to tarry, wait; for he will come at his appointed time, and will not tarry. We may crave for the coming of the refreshing season from the presence of the Lord; but take care, lest we make mockers instead of God-honoring professors.

Now, brother Temple, look over this, and if you think these lines are worth putting in your paper you can do so, after correcting all mistakes; and if not, all will be right. I have not written as much as I thought I should when I commenced, but I will stop.

I remain yours truly,
JUSTUS PARRISH.
N. C., Jan. 23, 1858.

N. B. In refering to the views of so many offered on the "parable of the Two Sons," some say Prodigal; but I cannot find the word 'Prodigal' in my book, as I remember of. So as brother Samuel Tatum seems to think that the 'elder son' is 'Jesus,' and brother B. C. Headrick seems to think he is 'John the Baptist,' I will say to the two brethren, in the best of feelings, I want both of you to give your views on the Ninety and Nine Sheep, and the Nine Pieces of Silver. I had been thinking that the 'ninety and nine sheep,' the 'nine pieces of silver,' and the 'home son,' meant the same thing, as there was no division between them as I could see. But I feel like I am willing to give up my idea for a better one. I have my thoughts about them, but they may not be right, and it is impossible for all to be right, but all can be wrong. So as I am no preacher, I would like to have the ideas of these two brethren, or any other, on the subject, and also put in the 15th chapter of Matthew and 4th v.: "I am not sent but unto the lost sheep of the house of Israel."

J. PARRISH.

☞ We hope brother Parrish will pardon us for not publishing his letter ere now.—May it be read with interest.—ED.

PRIMITIVE BAPTIST.

Milburnie, N. C., July 10, 1858.

Broth JOSIAH HOULDER (of Johnston Co., N. C.,) requests my views on the 22nd, and last, chapter of Revelations, 1st and 2nd verses, which reads as follows:

"And he shewed me a pure river of water of life, clear as crystal, proceeding out of the throne of God and of the Lamb." "In the midst of the street of it, and on either side of the river, was there the tree of life, which bare twelve manner of fruits, and yielded her fruit every month: and the leaves of the tree were for the healing of the nations."

To get fairly to the text proposed, it seems necessary to refer to the preceding chapter, (21st,) and there I find that the spirit of one of the seven angels carried John away, in the spirit, to a great and high mountain, and shewed him that great city, the holy Jerusalem, descending out of heaven from God. This great city is the bride, the Lamb's wife, the church of the Living God, "having the glory of God: and her light was like unto a stone most precious," (xxi. 9, 11) even Jesus the precious corner stone, as clear as crys-

tal. 12, "And had a wall great and high;" "I will be as a wall of fire round about her, and the glory in the midst." Then I understand this great and high wall to mean God, who protects the church; as, "a garden enclosed is my sister, my spouse, a spring shut up, a fountain sealed." This city having twelve gates, refers to the names of the twelve tribes of Israel. 13, "On the east three gates; on the north three gates; on the south three gates; and on the west three gates." These twelve gates, standing east, west, north and south, may refer us that God has a people in every nation, kindred and tongue, and an entrance or gate prepared for them all to enter in. 14, "And the wall of the city had twelve foundations, and in them the names of the twelve apostles of the Lamb."—"And are built upon the foundation of the apostles and prophets, Jesus Christ himself being the chief corner stone.—Eph. iii. 20. "And he that talked with me had a golden reed to measure the city, and the gates thereof, and the wall thereof." This golden reed I understand is the gospel of Jesus Christ, by which the church of God is measured and prepared by the Spirit to hold out measure. The measuring of the wall by the same reed, may remind us of the character of God as revealed to us through the scriptures of truth. "And the city lieth four-square, and the length is as large as the breadth," &c. John goes on to state the measurement, and says "the length and the breadth and the height of it are all equal." Then this is a perfect square—no difference—no big I's and no little u's, for they are all one in Christ Jesus; for which Jesus prayed—that they might be one, even as he and his Father are one. Thus a description is given of the precious stones laid in the wall.

23, "And the city had no need of the sun, neither of the moon, to shine in it: for the glory of God did lighten it, and the lamb is the light thereof;" which points to the city or church of God triumphant, when all the elect shall be gathered together in one body, and Jesus Christ its head; where the gates of it shall not be shut at all by day, for there shall be no night there." "And there shall in no wise enter into it any thing that defileth, neither whatsoever worketh abomination, or maketh a lie: but they which are written in the Lamb's book of life."

I have referred to the 21st chapter in order to get fairly at the allusion of the word *it*, mentioned in the text; so I now proceed with my views on the text which brother Houlder and sister Boothe request them on, (for sister Boothe also sent the same request.) But it is a little singular that this brother and this sister of the house-hold of faith, who reside so far apart, should have the same subject on their minds at or about the same time, being near the same age—about eighty years old. Surely they feel like their pilgrimage in this world is near to a close, and want to hear something about their eternal home in heaven. When they must lay down their mortal form, may God grant them a happy exchange.

Now for the text: "And he (the angel) shewed me a pure river of water of life, clear as crystal, proceeding out of the throne of God and the Lamb." This river I understand to mean the grace of God comparitively to a river, owing to its abundance of water to supply a hundred and forty and four thousand, sealed of the twelve tribes of Israel, and beside these an innumerable multitude—all supplied of it, and yet it is full, so that there is a continual invitation to drink.—"Eat, O friends; drink, yea, drink abundantly, O belov-ed." Then this water is free to God's beloved, and none other. This river ushures out of the throne of God and the Lamb. The throne I understand to be the sovereign power and dignity of God, to do all his pleasure according to his own purpose and choice, independent of any other source. "He that sitteth on the throne, shall reign in righteousness," &c., according to the covenant, according to the redemption by Jesus Christ to the adoption of children by grace—a free and unmerited favor bestowed on the undeserving.— "I will be merciful to their unrighteousness, and their sins and iniquities will I remember no more again for ever." "If the Son therefore shall make you free, ye shall be free indeed." Then this river is as clear as crystal, which proceeds out of the throne of God and the Lamb; not a mote or a blemish is to be seen in it—perfectly free from injustice, or want of virtue and power to make its way to the vessels of mercy afore prepared unto glory. Although some are endeavoring to muddy it with a general atonement and special application; others with a general application, and the availibility depends on whether the sinner strives with the Holy Spirit; others, that God has done all he can until the sinner reforms his life and grounds the arms of rebellion, and comes to God for salvation; others, by the doctrine of Universalianism, that the sinner finally gets to heaven by the amount of its own suffering according to the amount of sin; another, that God hath divested the power in man to forgive sin for money, and another with his altar or anxious seats: but the whole of these combined together cannot muddy or produce a defect in the cleanness of this river, for it progresses with such power that it throws off every obstacle thrown in its way, so that it is impossible to deface it—it admits of no such mixtures as blots and blemishes—no other practices but that which it teaches. As to ordinances, nothing can alter or deface it; if sprinkling and pouring is resorted to, it discards it. If building founts to baptize in, so that the minister stands out of the water instead of going down into it and coming up out of it, is not valid. This river is too pure to admit of a compromise with error. It is too pure to be mixed with any thing different from the righteousness of its own—it is so perfect; and in fact, this river is entirely different from all others.

Sister Boothe, you have, in the course of life, had your garment (literally) stained or blotched to its entire deface with something which could not be well removed with our common water. But this river that proceeds out of the throne of God and the Lamb, clear as crystal, is quite of a different nature; its efficacy is such that it removes all filthy blotches, stains, wrinkles or any such thing, with certainty, and will never more return, For what the Lord doeth he doeth for ever.—"That he might sanctify it to himself a glorious church, not having spot or wrinkle, or any such thing, but that it should be holy and without blame." Then the soul's garment is washed in the blood of the Lamb and made white; but to wash the body's garment, literally, we could never begin to make it white. But not so with the water of this river of grace.—"Purge me with hyssop, and I shall be clean; wash me, and I shall be whiter than snow," (that is, the soul.) "For it is the blood of Jesus Christ that cleanses us from all sin." The soul that is born of God doth not sin: it cannot sin, because it is born of God; it cannot sin, because his seed remaineth in him. "Ye are no more under the law, but under grace; and ye are kept by the power of God through faith unto salvation, ready to be revealed at the last time.

But this river of water possesses properties in making a cure of a certain disease that ever has surpassed the skill of all earthly physicians,—born-blind. It never fails when applied to the born-blind, to cause them to see. This the Jews acknowledged. Jesus, after applying the clay, made of spittle, told the man that was born blind, to go to the pool of Saloam and wash; and he did so, and he came, seeing. We were all born blind, in nature, to the things of the Spirit, and cannot discern the things of the Spirit, because they are spiritually discerned," &c. "There is a river, the streams whereof make glad the city of God." "In the midst of the street of it, (the city,) and on either side of the river, was there the tree of life."

"In the midst of the street of it." I know not better how to apply this than to that of the heart; and as there are more than one street to a city, so there are to the several points of doctrine comprised in the Gospel of God, and in either is Christ found; so in the whole and in the street of the city, the main cardinal point is the conveyance as a pass-way in which the inhabitants walk or travel, as we walk by faith and not by sight, and faith embraces Christ, the tree of life, in whom we live and have our being. By this faith in the Son of God we live, and by it, the hand of faith, we receive spiritual food from every part of the Gospel of Christ, as he is in the midst of the city, the Church of the Living God.—"For by grace are ye saved, through faith, and that not of yourselves: it is the gift of God; not of works, lest any man should boast." The whole city draws by faith from every part of the Gospel ot Christ's spiritual food,—and why should they not, when Christ, as the tree of life, is formed in us the hope of glory.?—"I in you and you in me, and I in the Father." Then he is in the midst of the Church of God. Then He is the beginning, middle and the end of our soul's salvation—the first and the last.

"And on either side of the river was there the tree of life." In the first place, on the side of the river—on the prophetic and ceremonial side—he, Christ, was there, and so was this river in the covenant, types and shadows, and believed on with the faith that wrought works as a living faith, in whose hearts was the tree of life until John; and on the Gospel side of the river of grace this tree of life is there, and in the midst of the street, or hearts, is he there; and the same spirit of life in Christ Jesus that makes us free from the law of sin and death, made all the saints free before the coming of Christ. And take it all in all, he ever will be in the midst of his Church as her life and wisdom, and righteousness, and sanctification, and redemption—as her shield and hiding place from the storms of this life.

But again: This tree of life is on the time-side as the only object of worship and adoration—who gives his people of the river of water of life, and says to them, "But whosoever drinketh of the water that I shall give him, shall never thirst; but the water that I shall give him shall be in him a well of water springing up into everlasting life." This is the same water of the river that is clear as crystal, and proceeds out of the throne of God and the Lamb. But this tree of life is on eternity's side, and when the saints that have gone home—to their home of eternal repose —there they have this tree of life in eternity, and there also is the river of water of life to drink in eternal plenty and pleasure, as they will never thirst any more in the midst of this plentiful and flowing fountain.—"They shall hunger no more, neither thirst any more; neither shall the sun light on them, nor any heat." For the Lamb, which is in the midst of the throne, shall feed them, and shall lead them unto living fountains of waters: and God shall wipe away all tears from their eyes." While, at the same moment, the saints on the time-side have the same tree of life giving them water that shall spring up into everlasting life, while the saints on eternity's side are worshipping God, the saints on earth are worshipping him too; and while the saints on time's side are singing praises to God, the saints are also singing praises to Him on eternity's side. So we may safely conclude that this tree of life is in heaven and with the saints on earth at the same time. Then he is on either side of the river, "which bear twelve manner of fruits,"—the twelve patriarchs, the twelve apostles of the Lamb, and twelve times twelve the hundred and forty and four thousands, which brings it into manner of fruits, in this, as well as the twelve oxens, which bear up the molten sea, with their hinder parts under it, and their faces outward, three to the east, west, north and south. This molten sea, I understand to refer us to the Gospel of Christ; and the oxens, the ministers of Christ; their hinder parts, their fleshly nature, to which it is only a burden; for the spirit truly is willing, but the flesh is weak:" their faces pointing to the east, west, north and south, is in accordance to the commission, "Go ye into all the world, and preach the gospel to every creature," &c. Then this tree of life has borne the twelve patriarchs, all the Prophets and Apostles, and as innumerable multitude as the sand on the sea-shore, so that "no man can number.

"And yielded her fruit every month." Under this division of the text, I come to a decisive point of that faith through which we are saved, even the faith of God's elect, whithout which we have not the spirit of Christ, and with it we are saved and have both the Father and Son. This is a matter in which all God's children are concerned, more or less.

"Am I His, or am I not!"

I will try to bring the doctrine so plain that the babes in Christ can see and acknowledge its truth. First, The tree of life which I have been speaking of, I understand to represent Jesus Christ, who has "carried the lambs in his bosom." This I believe he did in the days of old. Then I am informed that the Church of Christ was in him before the foundation of the world by gift, purpose and choice.— "According as he (God) hath chosen us in him before the foundation of the world, that we should be holy and without blame before him in love." Reader, is this your faith? and have you a love for it? If your faith works by love and purifies the heart from error, all is right; Eph. i. 4.

It is necessary to prove that Jesus Christ is the elect.—"Wherefore also it is contained in the scripture, Behold, I lay in Sion a chief corner stone, elect, precious: and he that believeth on him shall not be confounded."—1st Pet. i. 6. This elect here spoken of is Christ. Again, "Behold my servant, whom I uphold: mine *elect*, in whom my soul delighteth: I have put my Spirit upon him; he shall bring forth judgment to the Gentiles."—Isa. xlii. 1. This also proves that Christ is the elect. Need

no more texts to the point; so I pass on now to show that the Church of God are the elect of God.—"Chosen in Christ before the world was." "Elect according to the foreknowledge of God the Father, through sanctification of the spirit unto obedience and sprinkling of the blood of Jesus Christ; grace unto you, and peace be multiplied." This not only shows the manner when elected, but shows how the elect church shall be brought forth spiritually and saved from sin, excluding any works of the sinner as in point of merit. It is through sanctification of the Spirit and the sprinkling of the blood of Jesus Christ, and not by the works of righteousness that we might do. Again, "Who hath saved us and called us with an holy calling; not according to our works, but according to his own purpose and grace given us in Christ Jesus before the world began." Thus you will see that, in God's purpose and foreknowledge, the elect, chosen of God, were saved, and grace given them before the world began. Again, "But we are bound to give thanks alway to God for you, brethren, beloved of the Lord, because God hath from the beginning chosen you to salvation through sanctification of the Spirit and belief of the truth."

Question: Do you, brethren, believe the above passages of scripture to be true? and do you lo e to believe it? Is it spiritual food tov your souls? If so, I believe you are members or fellow-citizens of the city of God, and are no more strangers and foreigners. Having brought forward a sufficiency of evidence to prove Christ and his Church both elected, I shall next argue the cause consistent with common sense and reason.

"Verily, verily, I say unto you, Except a corn of wheat fall into the ground and die, it abideth alone: but if it die, it bringeth forth much fruit."—John xii. 24. This is a wonderful argument of Jesus to establish the doctrine of all the corn that the grain that died brought forth was virtually in the corn before it died, and after it dies it bringeth forth much fruit. I understand the corn or wheat which falls into the ground and dies, is alluding to Christ himself, and that before he died upon the cross all the seed of Abraham that ever was brought forth, or ever will be, was in him by gift, as the lot of his inheritance. There would be no need of choosing a seed to plant if it did not bring forth after itself or kind, and if it brings forth after itself, it is a strong argument that what it putteth forth was virtually in it by purpose before. Christ is called an apple-tree as well as the tree of life; and every apple that the tree bringeth forth was in it before, or it could not be in it at all. The tree bearing fruit will bear after its kind. Hence is the choice of fruit trees, because of its fruit. This must be admitted—that all the fruit it ever bears is the same equality from first to last, which proves that it was in the tree before. And as to its putting forth, it is the tree that puts forth the fruit, and not the fruit itself. "First make the tree good and the fruit will be good, but a corrupt tree cannot bring forth good fruit. But Jesus Christ, by the Holy Spirit or divine sap, puts forth in its time, but by his quickening power significant of that divine Spirit that quickeneth, a swelling desire for righteousness and holiness, being killed to the love of sin, and in place thereof has a love for righteousness. The Lord opens the eyes of the understanding to see a beauty in holiness and to its seeing itself a poor lost sinner, and it swells with grief and mourns over its lost condition. "Blessed are they that mourn, for they shall be comforted." This is why quickened sinners, at times, feel almost like their heart and breast surely will burst, and sometimes feel so sin-sick and sin-burdened that they can hardly go. Hence said Jesus, "Come unto me, all ye that are weary and heavy laden, and ye shall find rest to your souls." By the influence of the spiritual sap of this tree of life, the quickened sinner is brought into a panting position,—"Give me Jesus, or I die." "As pants the heart after the water-brook, so pants my soul after Thee, O God."—Following their daily occupation. This panting of soul, (though not a word spoke carries in it, God, be merciful to me, a poor lost sinner! Lord, canst Thou cast an eye of mercy on such a poor sinner as I am, The Spirit making intercessions with groanings that cannot be uttered until humbled down at the feet of mercy,—cut off of all dependence on any thing they can do—concluding that God is angry with them; no friend on earth to appeal to for relief. This is a dark time with the soul; and as it is most common for the buds and blossoms to appear in the morning, so "weeping may endure for a night, but joy cometh in the morning." So it is with the truly awakened sinner,—humbled completely, believing himself to be a poor, lost, condemned sinner—not worthy of God's notice, and views his prospects for life and salvation as dark as mid-night—just where God will have him—preparatory to the frank acknowledgment that it is all of grace, and that salvation is of the Lord, experimentally! Then the tree puts forth the blossom of faith, with all its sweet fragrance and beauty, to the unexpected joy, praise and thanksgiving to God. Now, as Satan makes false deliverances, I must here be particular in the putting forth "of the tree of life," or the yielding of her fruit. It produces a new aspect upon almost every thing it looks at, even the shining of the sun, the expanded heavens above, the beasts of the field, the trees of the forest, and its own flesh looks different—with a new, sweet and calm serenity of sorrow beyond the expression of the tongue of clay. Now for the proof that this is the putting forth of the tree of life.—"Therefore, if any man be in Christ, he is a new creature: old things are passed away; behold, all things are become new."—2nd Cor. v. 17. Now, there is no mistake in this ⬤dence; if you have experienced the truth of this new feeling and view of things, I believe you have passed from death unto life, even the life of the tree of life, and are born of him, who has borne unto you the fruit of faith to lay hold on eternal life. Again, "And Jesus said, Verily I say unto you, Except ye be converted, and become as little children, ye shall not enter into the kingdom of heaven."—Matt. xviii. 3. Now, have you any experience of becoming as a little child, as to helplessness to initiate yourselves into the favor of God by any thing you could do? If so, you are borne by the tree of life. But you may have thought that you always would remain in this happy condition as you felt when your blossom of deliverance opened; but alas! the scene is changed from what you expected. The bloom does not long remain in its sweet and flourishing state before the leaves of it begin to faid and dry up—similar to Isaac's weaning time, when Ishmael mocked him. Those heavenly sensations measurably subside—doubts and fears arise, and you fear that it is all false, and that there is no reality in your thought of deliverance from sin. And now efforts are being made to get back your distress, feeling willing to suffer more, but you have forgotten your former distress. The soul thinks that, if it were born of the Spirit, if it could get another such manifestation, it would, for the future, take better care and not let it go or pass off so again. Now, in the drying up of the bloom, you will see the little fruit begin to grow while learning, "the just shall live by faith," and not altogether by good feelings. Therefore there is a growth in grace and in the knowledge of the truth. Hence, this tree is to bear fruit all the year; and there are always on it blossoms—some shedding, some young, some middle-aged, and others ripe or old, just ready to fall (their bodies) in the cold, icey arms of death, to go home to their Heavenly Father. Of the latter, brother Houlder and sister Boothe may feel that they are just ready to fall into the death of their bodies. O! brethren, just stand off at some humble point, and take a retrospective view of this tree of life on either side of the river and view the wondrous scene of this tree, yielding her fruit once a month, (that is perpetual,) and never ceases as long as time exists—yielding for her (the church) the fruit of praise, the fruit of hope, the fruit of prayer and obedience, love, joy, peace, long-suffering, gentleness, goodness, faith, meekness and temperance in this world, and in the world above, the praise of the spirits of just men made perfect—all hanging or leaning upon her beloved, without a discordant note among the whole family of God, because they have, and will have, received of the divine sap or nature of the tree of life; all taught in the school of Christ: and he never teaches some one way and some another to the confliction with each other, but he teaches them, "One Lord, one Faith, one Baptism." This is the reason why we, who never saw each other with our natural eyes, love each other. They all freely attribute their salvation to free and sovereign grace, and not of the works of righteousness which we can do; for all our righteousness is as filthy rags before God; but His children are delighted with the imputed righteousness of Jesus Christ.—"Blessed is the man to whom the Lord imputeth righteousness without works."

"And the leaves of the tree were for the healing of the nations." The leaves of the tree may represent to us the external morality of the Church of God. Christ says, "I am the vine, ye are the branches, and although the leaves are put forth by the tree, yet they are generally seen on the limbs or branches. So the children of God should let their light so shine before others that they may behold their good works and glorify our Father which is in heaven. They are as a city set on a hill that cannot be hid. Moreover, God's ministers in particular, are the salt of the earth—in dispensing of the Gospel of Christ; it has a special effect to the Church of God, while it has a more moral effect on men and women that perhaps nothing else could affect. In this way is the nations of the earth healed of, or from, a more degrading state of darkness and insensibility, to the Being of the Creator and Preserver of nations. Although it does not make all the human family christians, yet it has a certain amount of restraint on the wicked in moralizing them. This, I think, is observable to all of observation. I do not believe that the leaves possess any regenerating properties in them, but do justify the inward life's existence as an honorable and beneficial influence. The Gospel preached, the earnest contending for the faith once delivered to the saints, has already had the effect of many reformations in different countries; other than that of regenerations, of course the leaves of Bible truth are included, or there is no word of reconciliation committed to God's ministers.

I might not have written to such length on this subject, if it had not been for the scarcity of matter for the *Primitive*; so I hope the brethren, who feel disposed, will contribute to its columns. I therefore hope my subscribers will excuse me for writing so lengthy an editorial. May grace, mercy and truth abound to you, brethren, beloved of the Lord.

P. S. There is another brother, whose name I disremember, and whose letter became misplaced, that requested my views on the same scripture. Though his name is not mentioned in my feeble remarks, yet, if I have written the truth, may he be blessed and gratified thereby.—ED.

The Abbott's Creek Union Baptist Association will convene at Flat Creek M H., Rowan County, N. C., about 4 miles south of Brinkley's Ferry, on the Yadkin River, commencing on Saturday before the 4th Lord's day in August next.

☞ The Editor having written beyond the expectation of the Printer, the Receipts are again unavoidably crowded out.

APPOINTMENTS.

ELDER WILIE PITMAN will, by appointment, preach at the Falls of Tar-River on Saturday 31st July, Sunday, Aug. 1st., Pleasant Hill; Monday, 2nd, Union; Tuesday, 3rd, New-Hope; Wednesday, 4th, Toisnot; Thursday, 5th, White Oak; Friday, 6th, Otter's Creek; Saturday, 7th, Sparta; Sunday, 8th, Old Town Creek.

AGENTS.

N. Carolina.—Hosea Fountain, Isaac Wright
Peter Jones, Wm. George, M. V. Wilson, Wm. V
Harris, Henry Shepherd, Elds. C. B. Hassell J. R
Croom, R. W. Hill, Josiah Smith, John H. Daniel
J. H. Keneday, James Wilson, W. M. Rushing, R
D. Hartt, Wm. H. McKinney, Aaron Davis, Wm
R. Hyman, L. Bodenhamer and Samuel Tatum
G. F. Nethercut, Ebenezer Morrow, Wm. Barnes
Simpson Lutta, Matthew Wilder, S. Hassell, Jesse
C. Knight, R. Ryals, Robert Hatcher, Henry Ste-
phens, Josiah Houlder, C. T. Sawyer, A. B. Bains
Wm. Welch, L. B. Bennett, Mrs. Esther Reece
Albert Cartwright, Q. A. Ward, Wm. Thigpen, S'r
James B. Woodard, Hudson Stephens, Josiah Coats
Daniel Turlington Green Bridgman, Edward W
Airs, Samuel Sadler, Hudson Stephens, Justus Par
rish, C. T. Green, K. L. Pender, Abram Wilder
Jeremiah Butts, Benj. Flemming, Wm. F. Bell
Alfred Horn, Wm V. Wilder, Wm. E Stone, Wm
Rouse. Sen'r, Allen W. Wooten, James W. Arnold
Elders D. Phillips, Wm. A. Ross, John Stadlar
and James H. Susser; E. G. Clark, James Car-
ney, Wilson Tilgiman, Jesse W. Leigh, Geo. Howard

S. Carolina.—Eld. Marshall McGraw, John H.
Whitmire, Stephen Langston, B. F. Thompson, W.
F. Hogarth, Willis B. Huckabee, H. Pate, Charles
Anderson.

Georgia.—Elders Jethro Oates, Eli Holland Isa-
iah Parker and Prior Lewis; Isham Edwards, Wm
Guy, Wm. H. Hogsett, Eld. E. Rimes, L. Phillips
Allen Brown, John McKinney, John R. Russell, Z.
A. Fowler, Wm. A. Nix, Daniel Gentry, Matthew
Caldwell, Jesse Pollock, Ezra McCrary. John Bar-
wick, James Haskins, James Hancock, Samuel
Steele

Alabama.—Elders Benj. Lloyd, R. W. Crutcher,
Troy T. Temple, James Daniel, Jeremiah Daily;
John Gray, S. Long, Stephen Cundle, F. Pickett,
Mrs. Sarah R. White, N. S. Stanaland, O. W.
Horn, Robert Allen, W. A. Vauter, Wm. Harrison,
Payton Wells, S. M. Matthews, Green Carver
Wm. M. Purifoy, James B. Miller, Thomas Colven,
Moses Rushton, Wm. E. Freeman.

Mississippi.—Thos. Young, David Harber, Thos.
L. Cotton, M. D., George Tubb, B. H. Pace, John
Francier Coleman Nicho.es A. W. Herring, A. J
Coleman, John Watkins, J. M. Reece, W. G. Rhy-
en, A. Botters, Robert McFaron, James Carter,
John Allen, N. Ward, Jordan Joiner, Henry H.
Burden, L. Sadler, M. L. Reynolds, L. Vanersdel,
R. Willis, Lai W. Cobb, L. W. Temple.

Tennessee.—Naum Powell, L. B. Stephens,
Wm. McBee, John Turner, Wm. Shelton, Wm

Gilliland, Dennis Tatam, John W. Reddick, Thom-
as Pittis, Samuel Day, Jacob Butcher, E. G.
Browning, Vincent Taylor, Anderson Brummett,
Joel Rushing, Wm. Swain, J. B. Reager, Peter
Smith, Dennis Springer, Samuel Thomas, C. J
Shelton, John W. Burge, John D. Matthews, L. F.
Evans; Elders George Huffman, R. W. Fain, Wm.
Hunt, John Parker, P. A. Witt, Hosea Preslar.

Missouri.—William Fewell, George Yoakum,
Wm. H. Mahurine, John Patton, C. M. Colyear,
Walter Bridgers, Wm. K. Evans, Henry W. Sel-
akeman.

Louisana.—Eaton Lee, John McCain, T. W.
Shepherd, L. R. Capers.

Indiana.—Alston Wyatt, Eld. Geo. Branson,
Milton Ballenger.

Illinois.—John Aylesbury, George Waggoner.
Ohio.—Eld. Hiram Allen, Andrew Cock.

Kentucky.—N. S. McDowell, Nicholas Darnald
M. Q. Ashby, Edmon Holloway, L. H. Davis,
Thomas Vass.

Virginia.—Rudolph Rorer, John S. Craddock,
Charles Hopkins, Thomas W. Walton, Wm. G.
Miller, Eelders Nathan Thompson and Silas Min-
ter.

Texas.—C. W. Dollahite, Jacob Mast, Jeremiah
Day, Alfred Hefner Isaac F. Wood.

Florida.—T. H. Hurst, Isham H. Bazzel.

TERMS.

☞ The Primitive Baptist is published on, or
about, the second and fourth Saturdays in each
month, at ONE DOLLAR per year, payable in all
cases in advance.—FIVE DOLLARS will pay for
six copies subscribed for by any one person at any
one Post Office. Current Bank Notes of as large
size as five dollars, where subscribers reside, will be
received in payment—A smaller amount than five
dollars, out of this State, is preferable in gold. Money mailed in the presence of Post Masters, and sent
to us, is at our risk. Letters and communications
should be distinctly directed to " Editor Primitive
Baptist, Milbarnie, N. C."

Job Printing

OF ALL KINDS, PROMPTLY EXECUT-
ed at the Office of the Primitive Baptist, about
nine miles East of of Raleigh. Persons who cannot make it convenient to apply at the Office in
person, will please leave their favers at the Store of
Mr. P. Ferrall's, where we will get them, or direct
them to Editor Primitive Baptist, Milburnie, N. C
☞ Charges will be moderate, and the work good.
BURWELL TEMPLE.